POSITIVE THINKING:

Easy self help guide: How to stop negative thoughts, negative self-talk, and reduce stress using the power of positive thinking, happiness, affirmations, and positive psychology

By: Brian Masters

Legal Notice

More from Brian Masters

Other books by Brian Masters
http://www.amazon.com/author/brianmasters

Follow Brian on Twitter
@brianmasterskdp

Table of Contents

This book is dedicated to those who desire to improve their lives and become more successful.

With the right knowledge and a personal commitment to employ positive thinking in your everyday life, you can achieve success on a scale you never thought possible.

I will show you how.

Free bonus

Thank you so much for taking the time to read this book. I know that by applying what you will learn in this book you can make truly amazing changes in your life!

As my gift to you, please accept a free bonus ebook aimed at making you a more confident, persuasive, and effective public speaker. The thought of pubic speaking is known to cause even more fear and anxiety than the thought of death! If you've ever been in a situation where speaking in front of people made you nervous, check out this bonus ebook *available now at no additional cost to you* and learn some tips that will help you next time around!

Claim your free ebook and get instant access by using the URL at the back of this book!

Introduction

Positive thinking is a strange thing. It is a key determinant in whether we succeed (or fail) in life. It is not an exaggeration to say that positive thinking is more important than almost any other personal quality. Positive thinking can be the fuel in the tank that propels individuals on to reach heights greater than anyone else ever thought possible. Someone who believes in themselves and is not afraid to reach for the things they want in life, no matter how big their goals may be, will have an infinitely better chance of success then someone who does not believe in themselves. Negative thinking on the other hand can be the barrier that prevents otherwise capable people from achieving the things they want in life. It can be the prison that confines you, separating you from your goals that may be so close and yet seem so far away.

But that isn't the strange thing about positive thinking. What is strange is that the sources of positive thinking in our lives can be so opaque and elusive. It can be so difficult to understand exactly where it is that positive thinking comes from, what determines it, and how we can get more of it. For all its importance in our lives, trying to take agency and control over one's own level of positive thinking is an awesome challenge. For those who wish they had more positive thoughts, the path forward can be difficult to see.

Stranger still is that at least from the outside, there sometimes seems to be no connection between one's own positive thinking and one's own abilities in life. We have all met the obnoxious, self assured hot shot who thinks he or she knows everything and in fact knows very little. And yet s/he appears to be brimming with positive thinking. We have also all met the shrinking violet. The person who shies away from a challenge and achieves only a fraction of what he or she is capable of in life because they lack the power of positive thinking to seize their opportunities and pursue their deepest goals.

How can it be that there is sometimes such a tenuous connection between one's abilities and one's positive thinking? What determines one's level of positive thinking? Where does positive thinking come from, and how can I get more of it? These are all legitimate and challenging questions. In this book, I will show you the answers to all of these questions and more.

Increasing your positive thinking requires understanding something akin to a secret code. It is not straight forward. There is no single answer or magic five minute affirmation. The way to build your positive thinking is to first understand the factors or "building blocks" that form the source of your thoughts, and then to launch a two-pronged approach of subjective mental changes and objective goal setting in order to make positive changes in each of these key areas. This is the positive thinking code, and this is the way you can achieve *real, significant, and permanent* increases in your positive thinking that you will start to notice in a matter of days. Let me show you this code so you can unlock your own positive thinking and live the life you want to live. Let's start now.

The building blocks of positive thinking

Positive thinking is based on certain ideas and perceptions that we have about ourselves and our abilities. The importance of each different factor (or "building block") varies a little bit from one individual to another, but for virtually all of us the factors that most significantly influence our natural daily thoughts include some combination of: the activities one participates in, the friendships and relationships a person has with others, a person's state of mental health, a person's state of physical health, and how a person understands the perception that other people have of him or her. Extensive research has shown that these are the most important factors in determining one's level of positive thinking, which means that a big part of building positive thinking is creating and following a plan to improve each of these factors. We'll go through these factors one by one and discuss how you can make positive changes in each area that will increase your positive thinking.

Activities

Thinking positively is influenced by the way you feel about your day to day activities. Note that the activities themselves tend to be less important than how one *feels* about them. There are plenty of wealthy and outwardly successful people (many working in law firms, accounting firms, and investment banks) who feel miserable and unfulfilled by the work they do and they pay a price in the form of scathing and intractable negative self-talk.

How do you feel about your day to day activities? Do you pursue things you are interested in? Do you have satisfying hobbies? Is your work fulfilling? Or do you feel dissatisfied with the things you do every day? Like time is just passing by without delivering much that is interesting, fun, fulfilling, or rewarding? Do you feel guilty or ashamed about any of your regular activities?

Take some time to really think about these questions. Think about the things you spend your time doing and ask yourself whether you feel good about the way you spend your time. Most of us have room for at least some improvement, and some people have room for lots of improvement. I challenge you to make at least one positive change in your activities, starting today. Maybe that means watching one less hour of TV per day (or getting rid of it completely). Maybe it means joining a new group of like-minded individuals, taking up a new sport, learning a language, starting a project you've been putting off, drinking less alcohol, or spending more time with friends and family. Pick at least one activity and write it down. Later in this book we'll talk about goal setting and how you can start working towards this improvement that you want to make.

By making a positive change in the activities you engage in, not only will your life be more satisfying and fulfilling but you will also be increasing your positive thinking by feeling better about the activities you engage in. Even if you don't have much free time, there is *something* in your life that is not completely satisfying to you that you can stop doing and replace with something that is more fulfilling, interesting, and worth being proud of.

Friendships and relationships

Friendships and relationships are another important factor that determines the level of positive thinking a person has. The expectations and feelings one has about their relationships varies from person to person. Some people only want a few close friends and will feel completely satisfied when they achieve this. Others may need a wider and shallower network of friends and acquaintances to be satisfied. Some people enjoy frequently meeting new people whether they go on to become good friends or not while this is less important to others. Whichever your preference is does not matter as far as building your positive thinking goes. There is no magic number of friends you must have in order to think positively about yourself. What matters is how you *feel* about your friends and your relationships, including whether you want more or less. It is important therefore, that you consider what the *ideal social life looks like for you*. Does it include only a few friends with whom you are very close and see regularly? Or are lots of acquaintances important to you? There are no "right" or "wrong" answers in this regard. Different people simply have different preferences for structuring their social life that is based on some combination of their genes and their social experiences. From the perspective of building positive thinking, it doesn't matter which types of relationships you prefer, only that *you know what you prefer* and that you take steps to achieve it.

Once you've figured out what an ideal social life looks like for you, compare it to your current social life. Notice some of the differences between your current social life and your ideal social life. Maybe you would like to have a few more acquaintances. Or maybe you would prefer if a couple of your acquaintances were better friends who you could confide in and spend more time with. Maybe you'd like to meet some people that are entirely different from your current set of friends. Whatever the case may be, you need to start taking steps towards that direction. By doing so you will start to feel better about your personal relationships and consequently you will build your positive thinking.

As with the "activities" section above, take some time now to think of one or more things that you would like but don't currently have when it comes to your friendships and relationships and write it down. You'll need this list when we get to the goal setting section of this book.

Mental Health

The mental health component of positive thinking can be one of the most difficult for people to understand and improve on by themselves. There are many different types of mental health disorders that all require different approaches. Diagnosing and treating serious mental health disorders is beyond the scope of this book, but what is important for you to realize is that from the perspective of building your positive thinking, mental health is something to take seriously. If you suffer from chronic alcoholism, clinical depression, schizophrenia, or a host of other serious mental illnesses then part of building your positive thinking needs to include dealing with these issues in healthy ways. If you have a serious mental health issue that you do not seek help for it will hold back your progress and adversely impact your life.

One of the reasons why mental health is such a tricky component to deal with from the perspective of building positive thinking is that for many people there can be a "chicken before the egg" question that arises, especially with regards to feelings of depression. Specifically the question is whether you suffer from negative thinking because you are depressed, or whether you are depressed because you have negative thoughts. In my research on mental health and in my experience coaching clients, I believe the answer depends on the degree of "depression". Feeling down and dissatisfied with aspects of one's life but feeling willing and able to start making positive changes (even small ones at first) is not the same thing as clinical depression. On the other hand, a sense of general hopelessness about life, especially one that has persisted for a long time and prevents a person from making any positive changes for themselves may be a sign of clinical depression. If you suffer from the latter, I urge you to meet with a mental health professional in your area who can provide appropriate screening tools in order to determine whether a mental health diagnosis is appropriate.

Physical health

I have noticed in coaching sessions that clients struggling with negative self-talk too often ignore issues surrounding their physical health. They do this to their own determent, not even realizing how key one's physical health can be to positive thinking. Please note that this is not *just* about looking good. We all have some level of vanity and so of course we all care about looking good and this is something that impacts our thinking, whether positive or negative, as well. But your actual state of physical health, not just how you look, is also crucial. Taking care of your body is one of the most important ways to respect, love, and care for yourself. Over the long term, there is really nothing at all that is more important than maintaining one's health as everything else depends upon it.

Consider your own current state of physical health. Do you eat well? Do you get enough exercise? Most of us have room for improvement in both of these areas.

The *minimum* recommended physical activity level for adults is 1 hour and 15 minutes to 2 hour and 30 minutes per week of aerobic activity and muscle-strengthening exercises for all major muscle groups at least twice per week. Are you hitting this minimum level right now? If not, what changes can you make in your life to achieve this level? Many people feel they "don't have enough time" to exercise but this is hardly ever true. Reaching just the minimum level could be achieved in less than three hours per week. If you aren't reaching these minimum levels, there is *something* in your life that is taking up at least three hours per week that is less important to your physical health and ultimately your positive thinking. Stop doing that, start doing some type of exercise that you find enjoyable. It could be walking your dog, playing a sport, or going to the gym. It doesn't really matter what it is, it just matters that you do it.

As important as exercise is, the truth is it pales in comparison to the importance of proper nutrition. Eating a good diet is perhaps the single most important thing most of us can do to improve our physical health. Consider your current diet and look for changes you can make to start eating better so that you can improve your physical health and ultimately your positive thinking. Onc small change you could make right away is to stop drinking beverages that contain sugar. What we drink has virtually no impact on how hungry we are and many flavoured beverage contain large quantities of sugar. We all know soda is bad for this, but fruit juice often contains similar levels of sugar as sodas making it a poor choice as well. Sugar filled drinks are just added extra calories that do little to satisfy us and contribute to weight gain, diabetes, and poor health. If you drink beverages that contain sugar, this is one easy change you can make right away. Another is to add more leafy green vegetables to your diet. Aim to have at least half of your lunch and dinner consist of vegetables, especially leafy green vegetables like kale. Making an effort to avoid refined and processed carbohydrates and eating more vegetables and intact grains and legumes is important as well. We really are what we eat and so having a good diet full of healthy foods is the single most important thing most of us can do to improve our physical health.

Finally, consider any habits you have that are destructive to your physical health. Do you smoke cigarettes? Do you often drink alcohol or use recreational drugs? If you are serious about building up your positive thinking, you need to take your physical health seriously. It is a key component that determines your overall level of positive thinking. It is easier to feel good about your life and confident in yourself when you are not your own worst enemy. Work to build yourself up instead of working to destroy yourself with tobacco, alcohol, or other drugs.

Take some time now and think of at least one area you could improve in when it comes to your physical health and write it down. You don't need to think of a specific way to improve just yet, we'll cover that under the goal setting section of the book.

Before I move on to the next section of this book, I would be remiss if I did not address the fairly popular idea that alcohol increases one's ability to think positively of themselves. Certainly alcohol does lower one's inhibitions and it can help people to do things they might otherwise be too scared to do. But those who argue that alcohol increases their positive thinking have a fundamental misunderstanding about what positive thinking actually is. Positive thinking is not achieved by consuming mood altering drugs so you can temporarily distort your personality for long enough to accomplish something you might otherwise have had difficulty doing. That is just a temporary change in your personality based directly on having consumed alcohol. Real positive thinking comes from within you. It is long lasting because it is a part of who and what you are and how you see yourself in the world. Whatever problems you have that are due to a habitual negative thought process, I assure you that just getting drunk is not the solution to this problem.

How you understand other people's perceptions

The last key factor that determines the level of positive thinking a person has is how he or she understands the perception that other people have of him or her. Note that as with some of the factors above like activities and personal relationships, it is the individual's *own subjective feeling* that matters. The actual perception that other people have of you could be different from how you understand their perception. In cases such as this, it is only your own understanding that matters as far as your positive thinking is concerned. For example if you are perceived by coworkers to be a diligent and competent worker, but you mistakenly believe that your coworkers think you are a fool, this will negatively impact your thoughts. Write down one at least thing you don't like about how other people perceive you (or at least the way you *think* other people perceive you). You might be able to base some goals on this later on.

Subjective/objective distinction

You may have noticed a theme recurring in many of the positive thinking building blocks above: many of them depend on your own thoughts and feelings rather than anything objective. For example it does not matter how many hobbies you have, or even what they are. What matters is whether *you personally find them satisfying*. Similarly there is no magic number of friends everyone must have in order to feel fulfilled with their personal relationships. Again, what matters is whether you have enough good relationships with people that *you are personally satisfied*. I call this the "subjective/objective distinction". The subjective is how you personally feel. The objective is the situation as it actually exists, regardless of how you feel about it. This is an important distinction as it unlocks some of the mystery surrounding positive thinking and how it works.

The fact that it is only your own subjective opinion that counts explains why so many outwardly successful, competent, good, and likable people can suffer from hurtful negative self-talk. I think most of us have met at least one person in our lives who we believe is performing far below their potential. It could be a student who is smart but suffers from crippling self-doubt, a salesman who declines a promotion because he doesn't think he's up for the challenge, the beautiful girl with lots of friends who only dates people who treat her poorly because she doesn't think she can do any better, or a would-be entrepreneur with a great idea who languishes in a miserable job because he doesn't believe he can strike out on his own. What connects all of these people, and maybe you too, is that their own subjective beliefs about their activities, their relationships, and how other people see them has become distorted from reality. They critique themselves too much, make too much of their mistakes, and don't pay enough attention to their successes. In general, they dwell on the negative instead of focusing on the positive.

If you suffer from negative thinking there is a good chance that destructive beliefs you have about yourself are at least partially to blame. This is especially true of the beliefs you have about your activities, relationships, and how others perceive you. I mentioned in the introduction of this book that we will use what I called a "two pronged approach". The two prongs are the *subjective approach* of cultivating a positive mindset and the *objective approach* of setting goals and employing mental triggers to change your actions. Both of these prongs are important for different reasons. Changing your actions using an objective approach is important because your beliefs may not be mistaken. You may believe that your friends disrespect you... and you might be right! Maybe some of your friends are not very good ones and you need to take action in the form of finding and developing new and better friendships with people who like and respect you for who you are.

But if your beliefs are wrong then changing your actions isn't the remedy for improving your positive thinking. This is where the subjective approach of cultivating a positive mindset comes in. If your friends actually like and respect you and you just fail to see it because of your own subjective negative thoughts, then the solution is to *change your pattern of thinking* so that you can break out of the negative illusions you've been believing and embrace new beliefs that are more positive, better reflect reality, and will ultimately build up your positive thinking instead of tearing it down.

Of course knowing whether it is your subjective beliefs or your objective situation that is contributing to your lack of positive thinking can be difficult. After all, false beliefs are by definition *beliefs*. You believe them to be true, and you just happen to be wrong without realizing it. This is the reason why we need a "two pronged" approach instead of merely a "one pronged" approach. You need to combine both the subjective and objective approaches I will now teach you. In the section that immediately follows this one I will introduce you to the subjective approach and show you how to cultivate a positive mindset. In the sections after that I will introduce you to the objective approach so you can change your actions in order to achieve more positive outcomes. Together these two approaches are a powerful method for building your positive thinking when directed at the "building blocks" we have already learned about.

The subjective approach: Cultivating a positive mindset

Cultivating a positive mindset through meditation is a helpful tool for dealing with problematic negative thoughts. At the very least, a positive mindset will give you a boost in your positive thinking that can help provide the motivation you need to set and work towards positive goals in your life. For some people, cultivating a positive mindset makes up a much larger part of the solution to conquering negative self-talk as they let go of their negative reactions and internal monologues that had been keeping them from seeing all the reasons they already have in their life to think positively. Whatever your situation is, I urge you to commit to trying the technique described in this section of the book at least three times a week for four weeks.

I have to mention here that I sometimes find clients of mine to be dismissive of the value of cultivating a positive mindset through meditation. I understand where this is coming from. I consider myself to be a reasonable, rational, and logical person and I know that sitting alone in a room focusing on your breathing while trying *not* to focus on your thoughts can seem silly. But I am sharing this technique with you because I know from personal experience that it really does make a difference. I don't want to stereotype anyone here, but I've noticed that middle aged men in particular seem especially unwilling to commit to cultivating a positive mindset. I want to share with you three quotes that actual clients have shared with me after one month or less of regularly employing this technique to help them cultivate a positive mindset. Two are from middle aged men, one is from a middle aged woman.

"I was so sceptical that things like breathing exercises and meditation could make any meaningful difference in my life... but they have! I have so much more motivation to take on my goals

now!"

"The meditation exercise you showed me really helped. Now I mediate every morning and when I finish I feel sharp and ready to take on the day!"

"Before I tried it I just assumed meditation was a waste of time, but I have to admit that I really am thinking more positively these days so something must be working for me!"

The fact is, cultivating a positive mindset really is helpful for a lot of people. The more you have fallen into habits of being overly critical, pessimistic, or negative towards yourself, the more you have to gain from this technique. Regular periods of meditation can help you to achieve a higher level of mental agility and lucidity. It can also help you to adopt a more peaceful and accepting attitude towards yourself, embracing positive thoughts while breaking out of negative patterns of thinking. All of these improvements to your mindset will help you to build your positive thinking and improve your life. Here is an exercise I like to use. I have personally experienced improvements in my own positive thinking using this technique and I have also seen it help my clients when I introduce the technique in our private coaching sessions. I encourage you to try this for 15 minutes at a time, a few times a week (preferably daily), for at least four weeks. Let me teach you this technique now. I hope you will try it.

The purpose of this exercise is to *not think*. This is surprisingly difficult. Our minds run 24/7 with so many thoughts that we have little control of or sometimes even little conscious notice of. If you suffer from habitual negative self-talk, some of the thought patterns you are engaged in are likely pessimistic and self-destructive ones. This is why meditation can be effective. It breaks the negative pattern, if only for a few moments. The goal is to awaken from the endless train of thoughts so that we can enjoy the rewards of a mind undisturbed by judgement, criticism, and worry.

You should start this exercise by sitting upright in a silent room. You can sit in a chair if you prefer, or on the floor. You can sit in the middle of the room or with your back against the wall. Do whatever feels comfortable, just as long as you keep your back straight and do not slouch. Take a deep breath in and slowly breath out. Do this a few times. As you are breathing, try to notice where your body is making contact with the chair or the floor. Take an interest in the smallest physical sensations you can that are part of the act of sitting. Notice the pressure, temperature, or whatever else you feel. As you become more aware of these sensations, shift your focus to your breathing. Again, try to notice as many little physical sensations as you can. Focus on what it feels like to breath. How it feels when your lungs expand and contract. How the air feels entering through your nostrils or your mouth and then exiting from your body. Anytime you notice you are thinking about anything other than the feeling of breathing, return your focus only to breathing. Do not scold yourself or be upset with yourself if you lose focus. You will lose focus sometimes. Meditation is difficult. Take notice of your thoughts and then just shift your focus back to your breathing. Do this for at least 10 minutes, preferably 15 minutes.

You will find, if you are willing to try this exercise and stick with it over the course of the month, that you will improve your ability to deliberately focus your mind only on the things you want to. You will reach the point where you begin to simply notice the thoughts you have, rather than be automatically affected by them one way or another. Completely ceasing to think during meditation is extremely difficult, but fortunately you can experience many benefits of meditation before you ever reach full zen-like mental mastery. As you become more skilled at merely noticing the thoughts that occur you will increase your ability to overcome your negative thoughts as you experience them in everyday life. You will be able to notice them and then shift your focus away from them, ignoring them and letting them fade into the distance.

The objective approach: The value of goal setting

Part of successfully achieving a goal is knowing exactly what the goal is. You are reading this book because you or someone else in your life needs help stopping negative self-talk and promoting positive thinking. I understand that "more positive thinking" is what you want, but simply setting the goal "think positively" for yourself is unlikely to be very helpful. That's because the best goals are ones that are measurable in a way that is at least somewhat objective. It can often be difficult to quantify one's positive thinking at a particular point in time and then compare it to one's thinking at some other time. This is even more true when someone is building up their positive thinking. Building positive thinking is a process, not something that happens overnight. I would simply be lying to you if I told you that it is possible to snap your fingers, say a magic affirmation in front of the mirror and enjoy completely positive thoughts in 30 seconds. It is not possible. Building positive thinking is a process with ups and downs. This is why it is not useful to make your goal "more positive thinking". It can be difficult to tell from one day to the next whether your positive thinking is generally improving because there are ups and downs and because feelings themselves are exceptionally difficult things to quantify.

For these reasons, your goals must be specific ones that admit of evaluation. You need to know whether you have achieved the goal or not. It is best if you pick goals that are based on certain events that either do or do not happen. You should also pick goals that depend only on your own actions and decisions and not those of someone else. For example "get Bella to be my girlfriend" would not be a good goal, as the outcome depends upon a decision from someone else; a decision that might be totally beyond your own control. A better goal would be "ask Bella to be my girlfriend" as this is a specific event that that you have direct control over.

Staggering your goals

It is also best if you pick multiple goals that are based over different periods of time. You should always have at least one very short term goal that you plan to accomplish in the next 24 hours. Your short term goal does not have to be a major life altering goal. The whole process of building positive thinking will result in major changes in your life, but the point of the short term goal itself is not major change. The short term goals are meant to work more like baby steps. They ensure you are always heading in the right direction every single day, thinking a little more positively with each short term goal you achieve. *A commitment to making and achieving small, short term goals is crucial to your success in building positive thinking.* It ensures you will not stagnate in your journey to improve your thinking or allow yourself to slip into old, destructive habits.

In order to choose a short term goal, think about a situation that happened recently that cause you to engage in negative self-talk. It is best if you think of an everyday sort of situation that happens frequently in your life, or at least is likely to happen again in the near future. Even if it is a small or otherwise insignificant event in your day, if it is something that gives you a feeling of diffidence it will be a useful basis for a short term goal. Once you've decided on a situation, think about how you wish you had acted and commit to following a course of action that is at least a little bit closer to what you wish you had done the next time this situation happens.

Example: Norman doesn't know many of his neighbours in his apartment building but wishes he did. Norman struggles with destructive negative thinking and finds it difficult to confidently introduce himself to new people and get to know them. He decides that next time he sees one of his neighbours who he doesn't know in the hallway he will simply say hi and smile, instead of averting eye contact as he usually does.

Another good way to choose a short term goal is to think about something minor that you want to do but that you've been putting off doing because it makes you feel uncomfortable. Make that your short term goal.

Example: Mary attends a morning meeting every day at her office. She often has suggestions she'd like to make but doesn't make them because she is not confident in her competence at work. This is caused by her repeated negative self-talk. Sometimes the suggestions she doesn't make end up being made by others and are met with approval from her boss. She decides that the next time she thinks of a suggestion to make in the morning meeting she will speak up and suggest it.

Using artificial situations to move forward in real life

One of the challenges in setting short term goals is coming up with enough of them. You need many, many short term goals so that you can always be moving forward. Even if the steps are only baby steps, the important thing is that they *are* steps and they *are* taking you in the right direction. If you're not taking steps forward, you are stagnating or worse, moving backwards and thinking more negatively than before. Therefore you need many short term goals so that you will always be moving forward, starting today. If you have trouble thinking of enough short term goals that you can achieve in your daily life, I have a solution for you: you can create an "artificial situation" for yourself where you can achieve a goal that moves you forward in some way.

Consider the example above with Norman and his neighbours. Inevitably there will be some days where Norman just doesn't see any of his neighbours around. On those days he could go somewhere else, to a coffee shop, or even just an intersection where people are waiting to cross the road, and say a friendly "hello" to a random person. This may feel embarrassing and it will certainly feel unnatural, but that is not necessarily a bad thing. The whole point of setting these goals is to pull yourself out of your comfort zone a little bit at a time. A good analogy for building positive thinking is building muscles. When you repeatedly push a muscle to do more than it usually does it must respond by getting bigger and stronger. Positive thinking works this way too. More than feeling embarrassed about doing something unusual and unexpected like saying hi to a random stranger, you should feel good that you love and care enough about your own well-being that you achieved your short term goal for the day and that you're making progress towards increasing your positive thinking. Besides, you can always do it as far away from home as you want where no one knows who you are or will ever see you again!

How you create these "artificial situations" is up to you but it is of course best if you try to pick things that make you feel at least a little bit uncomfortable. That is the point, after all. The exercise is useless if you do something you are already comfortable with. Maybe you wish you had the confidence to take singing lessons so you could eventually perform on stage, but negative thinking has held you back. You could make one of your short term goals to sing out loud for a few seconds while waiting in line at a grocery store. Maybe you struggle to be assertive enough to ask people to do things for you. Your short term goal could be to ask a random stranger to help give you directions to somewhere. You don't have to actually be going there of course, you can just get the information, thank the person, and leave.

Ultimately, the only thing that matters is that you do *something* that challenges your negative and limiting thoughts more than usual. It doesn't matter what the situation is, which is why I call it an "artificial" situation. Exercises like these can be a great way to ensure you never run out of short term goals and consequently never stop building up your positive thinking.

Setting bigger goals

In addition to your short term goal you should pick a medium term goal. Something that you would like to have the confidence to achieve in the next three months or so but haven't been able to in the past due to negative thinking. It is helpful if you base at least some of your short term goals on the medium term goal so that you are gradually working towards the goal, improving your positive thinking along the way. In other words, not all of your short term goals should be "artificial" ones (I imagine you wouldn't want them to be anyway, I know these types of goals can feel very uncomfortable!). Here is an example of how Norman from the above example might go about picking a medium term goal:

Example: Norman would like to spend some time with one of neighbours in the hopes that they might become friends. By acting on his short term goal and introducing himself to people regularly he is also working towards his medium term goal. Within three months he is likely to have met a number of new people in his building and be developing enough of a rapport with at least one of them that he could invite them to join him for lunch, coffee, a local event, etc.

Finally, in addition to your short term and medium term goals, you should also pick a long term goal. This goal can be quite a bit loftier than your short term and medium term goals. Once again, it is helpful if you base at least some of your short term and medium term goals on achieving the long term goal, such that you are gradually working your way towards the goal.

Example: Norman would like to have a party at his apartment next summer and invite many of his neighbours, something he has never had the self confidence to do before. By working towards the short term and medium term goals he has set for himself, Norman will be

41

building up his confidence and ability to think positively to the point where he can plan out the party and invite many of his neighbours.

Always having multiple goals to be working towards that are spaced out over varying periods of time is an excellent strategy for building positive thinking and ensuring your progress doesn't begin to stagnate.

Mental triggers

A very useful psychological tool for understanding the source of your thoughts, whether positive or negative, is called a "mental trigger". A mental trigger is a specific frame of mind, feeling, thought, or fear, that you have identified as one that often comes before your decision to engage in a destructive or undesirable action and that you have decided will remind or "trigger" you to follow a different course of action in the future. The idea is that you want to pinpoint a specific condition (typically a thought, feeling, or fear) that you know leads to an undesirable outcome (an action you take that you want to change). Let's consider the example of Norman from earlier in the book to better understand what a mental trigger is and how to pick one for yourself.

Norman was having a problem with persistent negative self-talk that led to his inability to develop better friendships with his neighbours in his apartment building. I asked Norman in a coaching session to think very carefully about the reasons why he would hesitate and avoid introducing himself to his neighbours or striking up friendly conversations with them.

"Well," he told me, "when I see people in the hallway they are always going somewhere. Maybe they are in a rush and don't want to talk to me. I don't have much to say that would be interesting anyway and I don't want to bother anyone."

Classic negative thinking! I know from talking to Norman that he was a kind person who was good to his friends and had a number of hobbies and interests. The problem for Norman was that when he would have the opportunity to meet someone new in his building he would start engaging in the line of thinking above. He would tell himself that he had nothing interesting to say and that his neighbour was probably too busy to talk to him. He would engage in this destructive line of thinking and it would lead to him ultimately avoiding his neighbours, saying nothing, and then going home and thinking more negatively then ever. Each time this process played out it just reinforced for Norman that he was not a confident person and caused his thoughts to become increasingly negative and damaging.

We talked about some of Norman's hobbies in that coaching session and Norman agreed that he had many interests that others might enjoy discussing. He also knew that if anyone was really in a rush and couldn't talk to him, they would simply tell him that and leave. Norman knew these things were true when he took the time to think about them, but his negative self-talk had caused him to engage in a destructive line of thinking when he was faced with a situation that required positive thinking, like meeting new people.

Norman decided that the thought "this person doesn't want to talk to me because they are in a rush and I am boring" would be his mental trigger. This is a good mental trigger for Norman to pick because it is specific and it commonly precedes the action that he wishes to change.

Using the mental trigger successfully means that Norman must be consciously aware of when he is engaging in this line of thinking. Over time, the habit of thinking this way had become engrained quite deeply for Norman. Lot's of times he didn't necessarily realize what he was telling himself that was causing him to avoid doing something he wanted to do, or that it was the same thing he was telling himself over and over, day after day, week after week. Developing a new habit of analyzing and recognizing one's thoughts can take a concerted effort and focus on one's own internal monologue. The process can be made easier by using the subjective approach of cultivating a positive mindset described earlier in this book, but it is still challenging. Norman made the commitment to pay attention to when he started engaging in this line of thinking and use it as a mental trigger to remind himself that actually he is a pretty interesting person, and if his neighbour really is in a rush then they will just tell him they have to go and it will not be a problem for anyone.

I hope this helps you understand what a mental trigger is and how to use it. To recap briefly, choose as your mental trigger a thought, feeling, or fear that you know is likely to lead to an undesirable action. Pay attention to when you experience this thought, feeling or fear and *as soon as you do*, remind yourself of the reasons why these fears should be ignored so you can engage in positive actions that help you achieve your goals, rather than negative actions that only further hinder your ability to think positively.

Conclusion

In this book I have discussed the key "building blocks" that determine the level of positive thinking a person has and I've introduced the key "subjective/objective distinction". I hope these discussions help you to better understand where positive thinking comes from. I've suggested a "subjective approach" that you can use to cultivate a more positive frame of mind and break free from patterns of negative thinking. I've also suggested an "objective approach" to improve your life in the areas that matter most for building positive thinking. I have only one final piece of advice for you, and it is the single most important advice I will give you in this book. *You must actually apply what you have learned in this book to your real life.* I guarantee this book will have done you no good at all if you finish reading it and then just go back to living your life as you were living it before you read this book. Love yourself enough to try the techniques I have suggested here. Commit to them for at least one month. I know from my own experience that *these techniques work.* I have seen clients who I have coached using these techniques transform their lives and think more positively than they ever thought possible. The increase in positive thinking is often noticeable within only days or weeks and becomes a *dramatic* increase within just a few months. You can use these techniques to increase your positive thinking too! But you have to actually do them. So put this book down, think about what you have learned, and put it to use. For the love of yourself, start right now.

One last thing...

My greatest passion in life is personal growth and development. I love to share the insights and techniques that I know with others in the hopes that they might benefit from them. I really hope the techniques in this book help you to build your own positive thinking and challenge yourself in positive ways so that you can live a better life. If you found this book useful I'd be very grateful if you could take just a minute or two right now and write a review of the book on Amazon or social media. It would really mean a lot to me. I personally read each and every review I receive from my readers. One of the best feelings in the world to me is knowing that something I wrote helped to make someone's life at least a little bit better. Thank you so much for your support.

All my very best,
Brian Masters

More from Brian Masters

Other books by Brian Masters
http://www.amazon.com/author/brianmasters

Follow Brian on Twitter
@brianmasterskdp

Free bonus

Thank you so much for taking the time to read this book. I know that by applying what you've learned in this book you can make truly amazing changes in your life!

As my gift to you, please accept a free bonus ebook aimed at making you a more confident, persuasive, and effective public speaker. The thought of pubic speaking is known to cause even more fear and anxiety than the thought of death! If you've ever been in a situation where speaking in front of people made you nervous, check out this bonus ebook *available now at no additional cost to you* and learn some tips that will help you next time around!

Claim your free ebook and get instant access here:

www.boostlifenow.com

Made in the USA
Middletown, DE
05 September 2016